The Heyday of Steam in South Wales

Derek Huntriss

First published 1996

ISBN 07110 2443X

Designed by Derek Huntriss

Published by Ian Allan Publishing

An imprint of Ian Allan Ltd, Terminal House, Station Approach,
Shepperton, Surrey TW17 8AS; and printed by Ian Allan Printing Ltd.,
Coombelands House, Coombelands Lane, Addlestone,
Surrey KT15 1HY.

Front Cover:
No 6003 *King George IV* waits to take over the up
'Red Dragon' from an unidentified 'Hall' which is arriving at Cardiff General with the train from West Wales in
September 1960. No 6003 was one of six 'Kings'
allocated to Cardiff Canton (86C) MPD at that time
following displacement from their West of England
duties by new diesel-hydraulics.

Rear Cover:
0-6-0PT No 3753 shunts at Cresselly Crossing,
Mountain Ash on 31 May 1962.

This Page: A shunter clings to the side of the loco as
0-6-2T No 5620 propels loaded wagons onto the coal
stage at Cardiff East Dock (88L) MPD on 31 March
1963.

All uncredited photos taken by Alan Jarvis.

Introduction

The dense railway network of South Wales, one of the most complex in the British Isles, was encompassed in an area of nine hundred and eighty-five square miles of hill and vale and operated in twenty major valleys having more than three hundred towns and villages with a total of nearly one million seven hundred thousand inhabitants. Within this area based on a mineral wealth, second to none in its day, grew one of the densest railway networks in Great Britain with up to fifteen independent railways operating.

The Taff Vale was the first public railway in Wales and was opened from Merthyr Tydfil to Cardiff Docks in 1841 as a standard-gauge line. This railway contributed more than any other to the development of the Port of Cardiff which eventually made it the premier port in the world for the export of coal.

This mineral was the most important, and profitable commodity moved for many years. To understand the volume of traffic moved, the town of Pontypridd, which was one of the bustling hubs within the South Wales valleys, can be examined. North of Pontypridd trains carried the coal from the Taff, Cynon and Rhondda Valleys and at one time it amounted to over 17 million tons annually. If this traffic was conveyed in train loads of sixty 10-ton wagons, this meant that a loaded coal train or an empty return passed through Pontypridd every eight minutes day and night.

As with so many areas of Britain, today's rail network in South Wales is not even a shadow of its former self. Economic recession, competition from motor transport, and the virtual elimination of coal production have seen lines closed and the number of trains dramatically reduced.

For the first time in colour this title takes the reader back to happier days in the South Wales valleys when the railways were operating under BR. Here they are illustrated as they were seen by the dedicated photographers, whose work makes up this title, during the late 1950s and up to the mid-1960s before BR eliminated steam traction in this area. The title is roughly divided into two parts. The first takes the reader on a journey up the South Wales main line from Swansea to Severn Tunnel and the second explores the valleys in a general east to west direction.

The author would like to point out that placename spellings and county names have been written as they appeared in contemporary railway timetables and other publications, which may well differ from the names which are in current use.

Bibliography

R. A. Cooke: *Atlas of the GWR — 1947;* Wild Swan Publications.
P. R. Gale: *The Great Western Railway — 1926*; Reprinted by Avon Anglia Publications & Services.
C. J. Gammell: *LMS Branch Lines;* GRQ Publications.
Michael Hale: *Steam in South Wales — Vols 1 to 4;* OPC.
John Hutton: *Taff Vale Railway Miscellany;* OPC.
H. Morgan: *South Wales Branch Lines ;* Ian Allan.
James Page: *Forgotten Railways — South Wales;* David & Charles.
James Page: *Rails in the Valleys;* David & Charles.
Paul Smith: *The Handbook of Steam Motive Power Depots — Vol 2 ;* Platform 5 Publishing Co.
Ian L. Wright:*Branch Line Byways — South Wales;* Atlantic Transport Publishing.
Magazines: *Backtrack; Modern Railways; Railway Magazine; Railway World: Steam Railway; Steam World; The World of Trains; Trains Illustrated .*

Acknowledgements

Thanks are offered to all the dedicated photographers whose work appears in these pages, in particular to Alan Jarvis without whose co-operation this title could not have been contemplated.

I must also give sincere thanks to photographers John Wiltshire, Trevor Owen and Bill Potter whose work complements that of Alan Jarvis in giving a broader coverage of the area. In addition to these photographers, I must also offer my thanks to fellow Cornwall Railway Society member, Mike Roach, for the loan of numerous text books on the subject, without which the captions could not have been written.

Sincere thanks also go to Ray Caston of the Welsh Railways Research Circle for sharing his in-depth knowledge of the subject.

Derek Huntriss

Camborne
Cornwall
December 1995

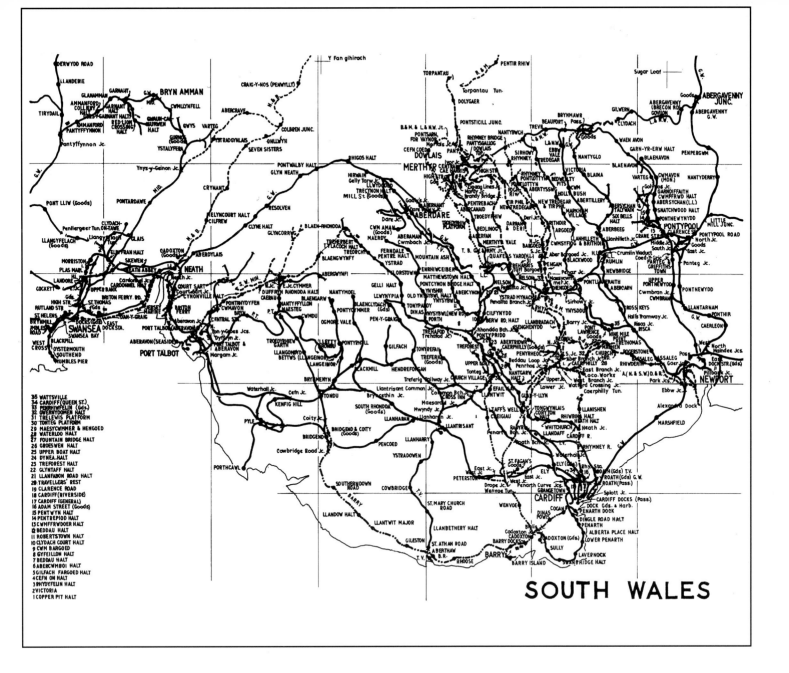

SOUTH WALES

Left:
Looking somewhat careworn 4-6-0 No 5054 *Earl of Ducie* prepares to leave Swansea High Street with the up 'Pembroke Coast Express' on 26 April 1963. Swansea was the only South Wales town to be served by three national railway companies. These were the GWR, MR & LNWR, each arriving after leasing or absorbing local railway companies. On 18 June 1850 the GWR opened their broad gauge line from Chepstow to Swansea and, two years later, its extension to Llanelly, conversion to standard gauge taking place during the weekend of 11 & 12 May 1872. The Midland Railway's entry came in 1874 via the Swansea Vale Railway and was completed with running powers over the Neath & Brecon Railways from Colbren to Ynisygeinon. The LNWR, which was seeking access to the South Wales coalfields, came via its line from Craven Arms which met the Vale of Towy Railway at Llandovery.

Extensive modernisation was carried out at Swansea High Street in the 1930s although the suffix High Street was dropped after the closure of Swansea (Victoria), the former LNWR station, in 1964.

Right:
'Prairie' 2-6-2T No 4110 brings life to Neath General at midday on 29 April 1964 following its eastwards arrival from Pontypool Road via Crumlin viaduct, Quakers Yard, Aberdare and the Vale of Neath line. The main line running depot at Neath was Court Sart, coded NEA under the GWR and later 87A under BR. It consisted of two roundhouses and had an allocation of over 60 locomotives, of which up to 15 could be outstationed at sub-sheds. When Landore depot closed to steam in June 1961, some of its tender engines were transferred to Neath, resulting in Neath having 'Castles' for the first time. Closing from 14 June 1965, the site was later cleared and used for playing fields.

Left: An unidentified bunker first 2-8-0T heads an eastbound coal train up the Swansea to Cardiff main line towards St Fagans, four miles west of Cardiff, on 12 April 1963. Behind the locomotive is the St Fagans branch, a chord built to join the Barry Railway main line at Tyn-y-Caeau Junction. Behind the photographer is the former Barry Railway main line, the site of which formed the base for a new link road to the M4.

Above: 4-6-0 No 5062 *Earl of Shaftesbury* heads a down express for Swansea under the Barry Railway main line west of St Fagans on 4 August 1962. A late-comer to the South Wales railway scene, the Barry Railway did not open its main line to Trehafod until 18 July 1889. By that time all the easy routes had been taken, and to reach its objectives, one branch alone had no fewer than three immense viaducts in the space of

about six miles. In 1913 the Barry Railway shipped 11,000,000 tons of coal through Barry Docks — quite an achievement for a railway that had only two small collieries directly connected to its system. In its final year of independence and not withstanding a major coal strike, 5,500,000 tons of coal were shipped in addition to the carriage of nearly 3,000,000 passengers.

Above: 4-6-0 No 4093 *Dunster Castle* heads a Swansea - Manchester express through Ely Main Line station, Cardiff on 6 June 1962. At this point the line passes between two well known breweries. On the right, behind the station buildings, is the Rhymney Brewery (formerly Crosswells) and on the left out of camera is the Ely Brewery Co. In the same vicinity as the station was a vinegar brewery, a bacon-curing factory, a jam factory and a paper works; the smell of the day depending on the direction of the wind.

Right: Seen from the footbridge leading to Cardiff Canton (86C) MPD, 4-6-0 No 5092 *Tresco Abbey* awaits departure from the Milk & Fish Depot on 1 October 1962. When constructed by the GWR the depot was used as carriage sheds and is today used for continental wagon reception. Allocated to Cardiff Canton on 27 October 1961, No 5092 remained at that depot until it closed to steam in September 1962 when it was transferred to Cardiff East Dock MPD. Completed at Swindon in April 1938, No 5092 was

officially a new engine although she could well have been described as a rebuild of 'Star' class No 4072 *Tresco Abbey*. Costing £5,165 for the engine and boiler, plus £778 for the reconditioned Collett 4,000 gallon tender No 2572. Whilst tender No 2572 was officially attached to her, in fact she had a new one, No 2741. Tresco Abbey stands on the Isle of Tresco in the Scilly Isles and after the locomotives withdrawal on 26 July 1963, the loco's two nameplates were observed on a cart belonging to the estate.

Left: Bristol St Philip's Marsh (82B) MPD's 4-6-0 No 1024 *County of Pembroke* has been coaled ready for duty at Cardiff Canton (86C) MPD in November 1960. No 1024 was completed at Swindon Factory on 9 January 1947 and cost £8,156 to build, a figure which included £2,187 for the boiler. The 4,000 gallon flat sided Hawksworth tender cost an additional £1,917. Withdrawn from traffic on 8 April 1964, her total mileage in service was 643,975.

Above: The main line running shed at Cardiff Canton was situated about half a mile west of Cardiff General station and was coded CDF under the GWR and later 86C under BR. At one time the depot boasted an allocation of over 120 engines but was gradually run down until final closure to steam from 10 September 1962. At this date the remaining steam locomotives were transferred to East Dock depot which had closed in March 1958 when its turns were dieselised.

In March 1961, 'Britannia' Pacific No 70025 *Western Star* is among a queue of locomotives waiting to access the coaler. The brick building in the immediate background is the Lifting Shop which was used for heavy repairs. By January 1963 the new depot was open and awaiting delivery of 10 'Western' class diesels. These engines together with 'Hymek' Type 3s were initially used for main line passenger duties.

Above: In the last two weeks of steam operation at Cardiff Canton MPD 2-8-0 No 2866 is being turned at the Leckwith Road end of the depot. The brick built structure was composed of a 28-stall roundhouse and a six-track straight house. The building on the far right of the picture is the carriage shed and is still in use for diesel multiple-unit maintenance and storage.

Right: On the final day of steam operation at Canton, 9 September 1962, 'Castle' Class 4-6-0 No 5073 *Blenheim* prepares to depart for the last time. Renamed in January 1941, No 5073 originally carried the name *Cranbrook Castle* when constructed in July 1938, the castle not being the mediaeval ruin we might imagine, but an Iron Age encampment one mile south of

Drewsteignton in Devon. Like much of Canton's steam allocation, she was transferred to East Dock, bringing for the first time 'Castle' class locos to that depot. The name *Blenheim* was derived from the twin-engined fighter-bomber used by the Royal Air Force in the early part of World War 2, particularly for sweeps over enemy lines.

Above: Taken at Cardiff General in April 1960, 0-6-0PT No 8723 waits in the centre roads whilst an immaculate unidentified 'Castle' departs with an up working. Any reference made to the steam locomotives that once operated in South Wales from the 1920s onwards must include the GWR 0-6-0PT types and their saddle tank predecessors. The sheer numbers of '57XX', '64XX', '94XX' and the earlier '1076', '1854', '2021' and '2721' types demand a mention. Whilst they cannot all be described here, the '64XX' is worth some attention. Derived from the '2021' class of pannier tank, they were intended for auto-train working in the hilly areas where the gradients were beyond the capabilities of the larger wheeled '54XX' class sisters. The majority of the class were always shedded in the valleys, their numbers, between 1937 and 1945, varying between 27 and 30 out of a total of 40 in the class. Lively and sparkling little engines they had an excellent turn of speed on the two-coach auto-trains for which they were designed. Their allocations were concentrated in the Newport, Cardiff and valley depots.

This scene in the heart of the Cardiff docklands, taken from the window of Stonefield Junction signalbox, depicts 4-6-0 No 5955 *Garth Hall* as it runs round to turn on a series of lines forming a triangle. Behind the photographer is Cardiff East Dock MPD. The buildings behind the locomotive are part of the GKN Castle Steel Works rolling mill. The cranes visible in the right hand rear of the picture are located at the Roath Dock.

Left: The low evening light in November 1963 adds a little colour to this scene taken at Tyndall Street , Cardiff as '9F' 2-10-0 No 92138 and GWR 2-6-0 No 6350 thread a triangle of lines before their next turn of duty. This movement was necessary because of the lack of turning facilities at East Dock MPD. On occasions up to four locomotives would wait to complete this manoeuvre together. At this time

No 6350 was allocated to Didcot (81E) MPD. Withdrawn on 6 January 1964, No 6350 had recorded 1,152,288 miles in traffic since completion at the Swindon Factory in May 1923. Initially allocated to Plymouth Laira MPD she had been allocated to depots all over the GWR system from Penzance to Birkenhead.

Above: A busy scene at Cardiff East Dock MPD on 30 March 1963 as locomotives blow off before leaving for their next turns of duty. In the foreground is 4-6-0 No 1010 *County of Caernarvon*. Running nameless after construction in January 1946, she was eventually named *County of Carnarvon* in December 1947, the correct name was bestowed in November 1951.

Gathering speed on the outskirts of Cardiff 4-6-0 No 7034 *Ince Castle* heads an eastbound empty stock working past Pengam Junction, Cardiff. Here were marshalling yards on both sides of the main line and a goods yard on the right. Beyond the signalbox running lines go off left to Roath Dock which join the Taff Vale Railway Roath branch at Dock Storage North. Today the lines on the left are still *in situ* and lead to Tidal Sidings and Roath Dock. Their operation has now been handed over to Allied Steel & Wire who work the line to Cardiff Dock with their own diesel locomotive. The first basin at Cardiff was opened in 1798 by the Glamorganshire Canal Co but was limited in use to small vessels. The Second Marquis of Bute opened the West Dock in 1839 and was followed by the opening of Roath Dock on 23 April 1886, the latter covering an area of 33 acres. The Roath branch closed on 6 May 1968 and today all that is left at Roath Branch Junction are piled up sleepers and great areas of concrete base strewn with brambles.

Two miles east of Cardiff General on the main line to Newport, a somewhat grubby unidentified 'Castle' class 4-6-0 heads an up Paddington express past Rumney River Bridge signalbox on 1 June 1963. The buildings in the background belonging to Connies & Meaden Structural Engineers have now been demolished to make way for a retail estate. The cooling towers at Roath visible above the buildings have also now been demolished. The marshalling yards which were accessed out of picture on the left have been removed and replaced by the Cardiff Freightliner Terminal.

Above: An unidentified '42XX' 2-8-0T heads along the up relief line with a steel train near St Mellons West, between Cardiff and Newport, on 10 August 1963. The flat roofed signalbox at St Mellons West is visible and its sister box at St Mellons East is just discernible. These wartime boxes constructed to an austerity design were used to control access to an inland sorting depot. Following World War 2 much of the landscape alongside the South Wales main line of the Western Region west of the Severn Tunnel has been transformed.

On the east side of Newport mile after mile of countryside was razed as the new Spencer steelworks of Richard, Thomas & Baldwin took shape. Beyond Newport and Cardiff British Railways had added a new flourish to the industrial canvas. In the postwar years the Steel Company of Wales created a 'boom town' in Port Talbot by its developments to the east of the original Port Talbot steelworks. The huge Margam plant and beyond that the Abbey works, each with its forest of chimneys and blast furnaces.

Right: The scene inside Newport Ebbw Junction (86A) MPD on 15 September 1963. This building was opened in 1915 and comprised two roundhouses under one roof with provision for expansion if necessary. At one time the number of locomotives allocated here totalled 140, the depot closing to steam on 4 October 1965. Also erected at Ebbw Junction during World War 1 was a 12 bay repair shop, although this was initially used as a shell factory. *Trevor B. Owen*

Commandeered from freight workings 2-8-0T No 5243 and 2-6-2T No 4145 pilot a failed 'Hymek' away from Newport High Street with a Paddington-Cardiff train on 21 July 1962. Only five months after this picture was taken, during the weekend of 8/9 December, the Western Region completed one of the most important stages of its Newport area resignalling scheme when the new centralised panel at High Street was brought into use. Whilst the final stage involving the transfer of signalling between Ebbw Junction and Marshfield to the control of the new box was not undertaken until early 1963, the commissioning of the new installation marked the completion of the major part of the scheme, which at that time, was already demonstrating its value in improved operation. Newport was an important traffic centre situated on the principal exit from the South Wales industrial and coal-producing areas to the South of England via the Severn Tunnel, to the Midlands through Gloucester, and to the North of England via Pontypool Road and Hereford.

The Motive Power Depot at Severn Tunnel Junction (86E) situated north of the junction of the Swindon and Gloucester lines, east of Severn Tunnel Junction station, is clearly shown in this view taken in August 1965. By this time the influx of new diesels is clearly evident, the only steam locomotive in view being '9F' 2-10-0 No 92238. A brick built six-track straighthouse was closed some three months after this picture was taken in October 1965. Although it was used by the Ford Motor Co for some years it has been subsequently demolished.

The practices for working the Severn Tunnel defined in the Great Western Railway's General Appendix to the Rule Book remained current when this picture of an unidentified 'Castle' class 4-6-0 passing Severn Tunnel West signalbox was taken on 9 September 1962.

The following statements, extracts from the Appendix to the Rule Book, implemented by Notice S1916, published at Bristol (TM) in April 1943, and subsequently published in the summer 1988 issue of *Backtrack magazine:-*

'*Passenger Trains* — Passenger Trains must not pass through the Severn Tunnel in less than six minutes.

'*Freight Trains* must in all cases enter the Severn Tunnel at a speed not exceeding twelve miles an hour, but the Distant Signals will be lowered for such trains when possible. Whilst running on the descending gradient the speed must not, at any point, exceed 30 miles an hour.

'*Guards* of Up Coal Trains are specially instructed to apply their hand brakes carefully when descending the Incline from Severn Tunnel West end to the level at the centre of the tunnel, to avoid the Drivers of Assistant Engines having to apply their brakes unduly in front.

'*Anti-Gas Precautions*

In the event of war gases being used by the enemy, special precautions will be necessary to prevent the gas being introduced into the Severn Tunnel through the ventilating shaft at Sudbrook.

'The Regional Commissioner, Cardiff (No.8 Region), will advise Sudbrook Pumping Station by telephone giving warning of a gas attack, and the density of the gas, immediately he receives the information through his existing organisation.

'The Manager of the Sudbrook Pumping Station will also act on his own initiative if the presence of poison gas in the vicinity of the shaft is suspected.

'A number of the Pumping Station personnel on each shift have been trained in anti-gas measures. Regular practices will be carried out by the Pumping Station staff wearing anti-gas equipment whilst performing their normal duties.'

0-6-0PT No 8445 leaves Pontypool (Clarence Street) towards Hafodyrynys with a train for Aberdare on 6 August 1958. The section of this line from Quakers Yard Junction to Middle Duffryn Junction was opened from 5 October 1864 and completed the line from Pontypool Road to Neath. From 1858 trains had run over the branch of the Newport, Abergavenny & Hereford Railway from Pontypool Road to Quakers Yard Low Level station and thence over the Taff Vale Railway to Merthyr, and from Neath to Hirwaun and either to Merthyr or to Aberdare, whence goods trains had continued to Middle Duffryn Colliery after 1856. Another branch was opened from the High Level station at Quakers Yard in 1886. *Trevor B. Owen*

Below: Situated on the main line from Newport to the Midlands and the North West, the MPD at Pontypool Road also served the Eastern Valleys and the line from Neath. Wagons carrying general freight and livestock, as well as the all-important coal would be sorted in the yards and marshalled into trains for distant destinations. The eight-track shed at Pontypool Road is featured in this view taken on 14 October 1962. *W. Potter*

Right: The second Pontypool Road station opened on 1 March 1909, and had an island platform, with a bay at each end. Here an unidentified 'Hall' departs at the head of a southbound Manchester-Swansea train on a very wet 1 August 1959. In complete contrast to this busy scene, today only two running lines remain, multiple aspect signalling controlling the area from Little Mill Junction. *Trevor B. Owen*

Left: A busy scene looking up the Monmouthshire Eastern Valleys line at Aberbeeg on 6 August 1958. The Motive Power Depot at Aberbeeg was situated about half a mile south of the station beyond the many sidings which formed the marshalling yard. During the 1950s it had an allocation of over 30 locomotives, including 0-6-0PTs, '42XX' Class 2-8-0Ts and '56XX' Class 0-6-2Ts. *Trevor B. Owen*

Above: An unidentified 0-6-0PT crosses the spectacular Crumlin Viaduct with a Neath to Pontypool Road train on 15 May 1964. This famous viaduct was designed by one of the cleverest engineers of the last century, T.W. Kennard, and the first piece of the wrought iron structure was laid on 3 December 1853 by Lady Isabella Fitzmaurice. A casket of new coins was buried under the 'Lady Isabella' pier, as it was known, at the stone-laying ceremony although no trace of this buried treasure was found when the pier was demolished. The last girder was placed in position on 17 December 1855 and the viaduct, which had cost £62,000 to build, was completed. However, it was not until 7 May 1857 that the bridge was tested, with six engines and a wagon, making a total weight of 380 tons, run on to it. Withstanding the test, it was declared safe for traffic.

Below: One of the most arduous tasks for locomotives in the valleys was the haulage of iron ore trains between Newport and the Ebbw Vale steelworks. When introduced in the early 1950s, the BR Standard Class 9F 2-10-0s were allocated to Newport Ebbw Junction MPD for this work. Here an unidentified member of the class passes Crumlin Low Level on 27 July 1963. Unassisted, one of these locos could haul 21 loaded ore wagons; the equivalent load for a GWR '72XX' 2-8-2T was 16 such wagons. On this day another '9F' was providing rear end assistance.

Right: Seen from Crumlin Low Level station, 0-6-2T No 6628 heads a Neath to Pontypool Road train on 31 October 1962. The last train over this line was hauled by 0-6-0PT No 4639 on 13 June 1964. On the front was a headboard with the words 'Vale of Neath 1851-1964' and on the buffer beam was the Welsh dragon emblem. Unlike many famous structures of its kind Crumlin Viaduct ended its life in a blaze of lights and glory. Towards the end of the summer of 1965 the viaduct was chosen to feature in the film *'Arabesque'*. Gregory Peck and Sophia Loren rode horses on to the then trackless viaduct while Alan Badel endeavoured to exterminate them by firing at the fleeing pair from a helicopter which flew between the piers of the viaduct. He missed and the two stars lived on to other triumphs, but the viaduct survives only on film. After the line closed, five companies attempted to dismantle the Crumlin Viaduct, including a German contractor, but the task was finally undertaken by Bird's, who built a Bailey Bridge and moved it along as each section was demolished. *W. Potter*

On 11 July 1962, 0-6-0PT No 3766 is seen from the yard of the closed station at Machen Church Road with the 7.7pm Newport-Brecon. Most of the original signalboxes and equipment on the Brecon & Merthyr were supplied by McKenzie & Holland somersault signals being the order of the day. The station at Machen Church Road served the district of Lower Machen, but it saw limited use and was unstaffed for several years before complete closure became effective from 16 September 1957. The southern section of the B&M was an example of a tramroad being converted into a public railway. Known as the 'Old Rumney', it was built to link the Rhymney Ironworks to Bassaleg, and continued over the Monmouthshire Tramroad to Newport. The tramroad was bought by the Brecon & Merthyr Tydfil Junction Railway Co, to give it its full name, in 1863, who then began to modernise the line, passenger services beginning between Newport (Dock Street) and Pengam on 14 June 1865, these being extended to Rhymney on 16 April 1866.

A bunker first 0-6-0PT leaves Trethomas with an afternoon New Tredegar-Newport train on 24 December 1962. Whilst most of the older stations on the B&M were plain and rendered in cement, their appearance being dull and drab, facilities at Trethomas, which opened in 1915, were even less substantial. From Trethomas the line was straight for 1¼ miles to just beyond Bedwas station where the line ran through the site of the local colliery. Passenger services from Newport to Brecon and New Tredegar were withdrawn from 31 December 1962, the yard at Trethomas closing from 16 July 1964.

Above: 0-6-0 No 2247 heads the 7.7pm from Newport to Brecon through the colliery at Bedwas on 19 July 1962. After passing the coke ovens at Bedwas, the line swung due north into the lower half of the Rhymney Valley. On the east side of the valley, there was no industry for the first few miles: the Rhymney Railway line was on the west side of the valley, serving the coal mines of Llanbradach from where, it was reputed, the

best steam coal came. After a further mile or two the site of the junction with the Barry Railway was passed, the Barry line had crossed the valley on Llanbradach viaduct. The next section of the line as far as Maesycwmmer was largely unspoilt, the station at Maesycwmmer being where the GW line from Pontypool Road and Neath passed over the route.

Right: After steam on all BR lines in South Wales had come to an end, the industrial scene typical of many South Wales collieries continued into the early 1980s. Here, Andrew Barclay 0-6-0ST 1091/06 *Lundie* is seen close to the former B&M main line at Bedwas Colliery in March 1968. The colliery and nearby coke ovens still providing traffic well into the 1980s on what was a single line from Bassaleg.

Left: The 7.7pm Newport-Brecon is seen once again in superb evening light, this time near Barry Junction (Duffryn Isaf) on 26 June 1962 with 0-6-0 No 2218 in charge of two coaches. The Barry Railway gained access to the Rhymney branch with the opening of its extension from Penrhos Junction on 2 January 1905. Whilst the Barry Railway's traffic was only coal trains, excursion trains from the Rhymney Valley and via the Merthyr, Tredegar and Abergavenny (LNWR) line to Barry Island operated over this route. Losing a certain

amount of coal traffic that was diverted from Newport to Barry Docks, the B&MR was well compensated by its receipts from the passage of traffic off the Rhymney Railway that the Barry Railway siphoned away from its former route to Cardiff. In addition to this the Barry Railway provided most of the money which paid for the doubling of the B&MR main line up to Abertysswg as well as the installation of additional signalboxes thus avoiding delays to B&MR trains.

Above: On 31 May 1962 0-6-0PT No 3661 brings a Brecon-Newport train into the platform at Maesycwmmer. Behind the train can be seen some of the 15 arches of Hengoed Viaduct carrying the Taff Vale Extension of the Newport, Abergavenny and Hereford Railway over the Rhymney Valley. Built in 1847, the viaduct remains to this day as an industrial monument, whereas the station has disappeared under a road improvement scheme.

Looking north at Pontllanfraith High Level on 27 June 1963 a bunker first 0-6-0PT heads a short goods past the former LNWR Pontllanfraith High Level Station signalbox. One of the many complex junctions in the valleys, the triangle formed at Pontllanfraith was where the London & North Western and Great Western Railways crossed and exchanged traffic. At this point three junctions existed within a matter of yards. These consisted of Tredegar Lower Junction, Sirhowy Junction and Bird-in-Hand Junction, the latter taking its name from that of a local public house, which happily still serves its customers. These connections were very important, since for many years the GWR used running powers to enable its traffic from the Aberdare and other valleys to reach the south of England by a less steeply graded and shorter route than that via Pontypool.

The Monmouthshire Railway Society's 'Rambling 56' railtour of 31 July 1965 toured branches in Glamorgan and Monmouth and was hauled by 0-6-2T No 6643. It is seen here at Bargoed station where participants have taken the opportunity for a photographic stop. One of the original Rhymney Railway stations of 1858, the station at Bargoed was a stone-built structure with the booking office on a bridge spanning the tracks. Several other Rhymney Railway stations were built to this pattern. The up platform was an island, the outer face mainly serving the trains of the Brecon & Merthyr Railway proceeding to Brecon. The Rhymney Railway became a constituent company of the GWR group on 25 March 1922, having passed from a penniless concern to become one of the best investments of its day.

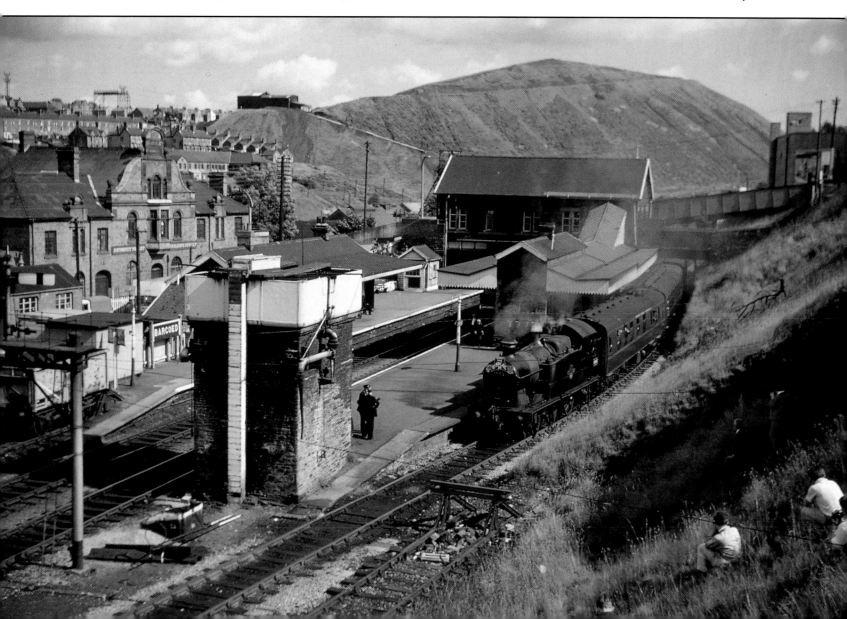

Left: Depicted in September 1963, the crew of 0-6-2T No 5660 prepare for their next duty at Dowlais Cae Harris. The Taff Bargoed Joint line ran from a junction at Nelson & Llancaiach on the Neath-Pontypool Road line to Dowlais and passed through several mining areas climbing over bleak moorland en route. '56XX' 0-6-2Ts operated a passenger service from Dowlais Cae Harris to Ystrad Mynach on the Rhymney Railway line, this service surviving until 15 June 1964.

Above: A scene remembered by many visiting railway enthusiasts — the Sunday shed bash of as many South Wales depots as possible, with little Sunday working, most depots' allocations were to be found 'On Shed'. Here, the depot at Dowlais Cae Harris is seen on a very wet Sunday 13 June 1964. Classed as a sub-shed to Rhymney and given the same code as Merthyr in BR days, the depot at Cae Harris was home to some half-dozen 0-6-2 tank engines which were used for working

both freight and passenger traffic over the Taff Bargoed Joint Line. Closing in December 1964, the depot had the unusual feature of depot separated from the coaler by running lines for much of its life. Here, 0-6-2Ts Nos 5602 and 5603 simmer gently outside the shed. *W. Potter*

Above: In the bleak moorland near Cwmbargoed, 0-6-2Ts Nos 5652 and 5650 power a freight for Dowlais Cae Harris over the former GW & RR Taff Bargoed Joint line on 1 August 1959. Today this line remains open to serve an open cast coal site. No 5652 was one of six members of the class allocated to Dowlais in 1950, the others being Nos 5653, 5666, 5671, 5674 and 5694. *Trevor B. Owen*

Right: 0-6-2T No 5687 approaches Nelson & Llancaiach station with a two-coach passenger train from Dowlais Cae Harris in September 1963. This station on the GWR Pontypool Road-Neath line (the tracks to Neath being seen on the left of the picture) was the junction for the Rhymney Railway's Taff Bargoed Joint line, a heavily graded branch built to carry imported iron ore inland from Cardiff to the furnaces of the Dowlais Iron works. This branch was one of the last haunts of four-wheel coaches stripped of all furnishings in the 1930s and reclassified to 'workmen'. These coaches which lasted into the early 1950s were often tacked on to the back of service trains and were used to convey miners travelling to several pits on this route, Bedlinog Colliery being one of these.

Far Left: This picture, taken in September 1963, depicts a '94XX' 0-6-0PT shunting the extensive yard at Aber Junction near Caerphilly. Northward along the former Rhymney Railway line, the yard was used for holding coal trains before despatch to the ports. From nearby Senghenydd Junction, a 3½ mile branch line to Abertridwr and Senghenydd was promoted to serve colliery developments. Opening on 1 February 1894 it had a frequent passenger service. Today at Aber Junction all tracks have been lifted.

Left: This splendid view depicting the complex track layout at Taffs Well was taken from Walnut Tree viaduct on 4 June 1965. In the foreground a bunker first 0-6-2T is at the head of a lengthy coal train. The double-track line on the right side of the picture is the Walnut Tree branch, formerly the Rhymney Railway main line. In the centre distance is the Cardiff Railway line to Glanllyn and Nantgarw and on the far left is the four-track former Taff Vale Railway main line from Cardiff to Merthyr. The stone building on the far side of the road bridge is the former Rhymney Railway loco shed. The second station to be built at Taffs Well has suffered several changes of name during its life. Becoming Walnut Tree Junction after the opening of the Rhymney Railway connection in February 1858, it was changed to Walnut Tree Bridge on 1 June 1886. From 16 March 1900 the station was renamed Taffs Well and closing for goods traffic from 27 June 1966, the station is still in use for passenger traffic. At the time this picture was taken the station buildings had some of the old charm and character left in them but today, these buildings, like most of the former buildings along this line have unfortunately been replaced by the more usual 'Bus Shelter'.

Left: Amongst the hills to the east of Nantgarw was Penrhos Junction, halfway point on the journey from Pontypridd to Machen. As we look west toward Aber Junction a '56XX' 0-6-2T passes with empties on 27 August 1964. In the distance to the left a bunker first 0-6-0PT waits to leave the Beddau branch from Aber Junction, the lines on the right leading to Caerphilly.

Right: Another view of the same train at Penrhos Junction, this time looking east. Set in a defile to the west of Caerphilly and midway on the journey from Pontypridd to Machen, Penrhos Junction was the focus of three railway routes. The first of these was the old Rhymney Railway main line, centre, whose 'Big Bank' ran down a 1 in 47 gradient to Walnut Tree Junction to meet the Taff Vale Railway. Next to these are the Pontypridd, Caerphilly and Newport lines running west to Pontypridd. Diverging left is the Barry Railway, and over the top of them all, centre are the abandoned piers of the Barry Railway's Rhymney Branch opened in 1905 and closed in 1926. The local trains serving the halts between Pontypridd and Caerphilly ran almost without alteration for 52 years. One curiosity was the Alexandra (Newport and South Wales) Dock & Railway Co's halt at Tram Road, just short of PC&N Junction at Pontypridd. All rail-motor passengers were deposited there and had to walk the rest of the way to Pontypridd TVR, due to the high charges demanded by the TVR for use of their station.

Penrhos Junction signalbox was unusual in having block bell communication with five other boxes in the directions of Aber Junction, Caerphilly, Walnut Tree (Taffs Well), Barry and Pontypridd. The actual boxes being in communication at any one time being dependant on the hour of the day.

On 18 April 1964, traversing the Taff Vale Railway's Radyr branch, a bunker first 42XX passes the box at Waterhall Junction with a loaded coal train for the docks. Behind the train to the left is the home signal for the Llantrisant No 1 branch which connected with the Llantrisant branch (Llantrisant-Tonteg) at Common Branch Junction at a point close to the site of the Royal Mint. The romantic barge-boarding on the gable porch and gable end of the TVR's box were given sympathetic treatment with a liberal application of British Railways' cream and brown paint.

After finishing her day's work at Ely Paper Mills, Robert Stephenson & Hawthorns' 0-4-0ST 7705/52 makes a special movement for the photographer in the snow on 16 December 1967. At that time Ely Paper Mills were owned by Thomas Owen Ltd, and are today part of the Arjo Wiggins organisation although all traffic is now handled by road transport. The 0-4-0ST was delivered new to the factory in 1952 and is still extant at the Welsh Industrial and Maritime Museum,

Above: After 36 years' service former Rhymney Railway 0-6-2T No 42 stands condemned outside Cardiff East Dock MPD on 25 August 1957. Built by Beyer Peacock for the Rhymney Railway as their No 46, she was delivered in December 1921. She became Great Western stock in September 1922 and like all Rhymney Railway stock, was found to be in a well maintained condition. *W. Potter*

Right: Also seen outside Cardiff East Dock shed on 25 August 1957, former Taff Vale Railway 0-6-2T No 390 awaits her last journey to Swindon for scrapping. Built by Hawthorn Leslie and delivered to the Taff Vale Railway in September 1920 as No 404. Spending all of her life working in the South Wales coalfield she was surprisingly sent for repair by the Yorkshire Engine Co in December 1925.

Considerable numbers of 0-6-2Ts from several South Wales companies were absorbed into Great Western stock in 1922. The 0-6-2T type had been introduced by the TVR in 1885 and by 1922 over three quarters of that line's locos were of that wheel arrangement. The Barry, Cardiff and Rhymney railways had all copied the TVR bringing a total of almost 400 0-6-2Ts into GWR stock. *W. Potter*

Left: 2-6-2T No 4145 takes the former Barry Railway line at Cogan Junction with a Newport-Barry Island excursion on 5 August 1962. The Barry Railway was opened for passenger trains between Cogan Junction and Barry Dock on 20 December 1888; the extension of services to Barry Town followed on 8 February 1889. Goods trains commenced running between

Cogan and Barry on 13 May 1889, the same day as the main line was opened to the junctions with the GWR at Peterston and St Fagans. The Barry Railway's greatest day was yet to come on 18 July 1889 when its main line was opened to Trehafod, the dock being opened in front of enthusiastic shareholders and their guests as the first coal trains trundled down the Rhondda.

Above: Also on 5 August 1962, Old Oak Common MPD's 4-6-0 No 5057 *Earl Waldegrave* heads a diverted Paddington-Swansea working through Cogan station. The diversion of main line trains between Cardiff and Swansea via Barry and the Vale of Glamorgan line during permanent way maintenance still takes place today.

Below: Barclay 0-4-0F No 2238 built in 1948 is seen in operation at BP's British Resin Products' works at Sully near Barry in June 1968. This loco became one of the last handful of fireless engines to remain in operation surviving until 1982. Today this engine is preserved in the Welsh Industrial & Maritime Museum in Cardiff. Fireless engines were used wherever there was a risk of sparks from a locomotive chimney causing fire or an explosion. Obvious places were paper mills, chemical plants, sawmills or munitions factories.

Right: 0-6-2T No 6658 heads a trip working away from Barry No 2 dock on 8 August 1962. The target board with a 'J' prefix indicates that this was an Abercynon working. Today this dock remains in use with five cranes still *in situ*.

Left: 0-6-2T No 5690 heads a westbound rake of coal empties from Aberthaw power station near St Athan on 29 August 1962. In the background can be seen the chimneys of Aberthaw cement works. In May 1969 automatic wagon loading and unloading on the 'Merry-go-Round' principle was introduced by the Western Region on coal trains from Blaenant Colliery, Vale of Neath, to Aberthaw power station on the Glamorganshire coast. One train of 26 32-ton capacity hopper wagons, giving an overall capacity of nearly 1,000 tons, made up to two round trips daily from the colliery to the power station. May 1970 saw the origination of four trains daily from Aberthaw to Pinxton, near Weston-super-Mare conveying fly ash for use on the M5 construction site.

Above: The Waterhall Junction-Common Branch Junction line was sustained for many years by one morning trip to Creigiau quarry. Here a '94XX' 0-6-0PT is shunting at the quarry on 18 April 1964. The principal outlet for the limestone from Creigiau was the East Moors steelworks in Cardiff, which incidentally was supplied with high grade ore from the Llanharry mine at the northern end of the Cowbridge branch.

Above: A Pontypridd-Cardiff via St Fagans auto-train working is seen arriving at the down platform of Tonteg Halt in August 1959. Tonteg Halt was built by the GWR in 1930, the double track in the foreground being the former Barry Railway main line. Situated between Treforest and Church Village, the halt came under the supervision of the Station Master at Treforest. Of the larger railway companies only the Barry had no depot of any consequence within the valleys. It never succeeded in penetrating far into the coalfield on its own metals and as a result maintained only a small establishment at Trehafod in the lower Rhondda, its principal purpose being to provide banking assistance for trains on the climb to Tonteg.

Right: 0-6-0PT No 9480 heads a loaded coal train away from Nantgarw Colliery near Glanllyn on 22 April 1963, the target board with the 'H' prefix indicating that this was a Cardiff Canton working. Originally sunk in 1910 by Taylor's Navigation Steam Coal Co, the colliery at Nantgarw was sold in 1924 to the Taff Rhondda. When the seam became harder to follow that owner gave up and sold out to Powell Duffryn in 1927. Then in 1947, Nantgarw Colliery and coking ovens were reconstructed and enlarged. With BR steam finishing in South Wales in 1965, steam enthusiasts concentrated their interests on the remaining steam-hauled industrial workings, the colliery at Nantgarw becoming a Mecca well into the 1980s.

0-6-0PT No 3730 passes Quakers Yard Low Level station with a down mineral working on 5 June 1964, the target board prefix 'C' indicating that this was a Cardiff Cathays working. The station at Quakers Yard Low Level had opened in 1858 and had exchange sidings with the GWR High Level Station which had opened in 1857. Today the area of the GWR station has all but gone, and a new housing estate has been built. In place of the ornate Taff Vale Railway station building there is now a British Railways 'Bus Shelter' type structure. Whilst the Pontypool-Neath line was best known as a cross-valleys link, it cannot be forgotten that the constituent companies' original aim was to reach Merthyr. The first branch was off the Vale of Neath section from Gelli Tarw Junction, between Aberdare and Hirwaun and the second to reach Merthyr, built jointly by the Great Western and Rhymney Railways. It deviated a little to the west of Quakers Yard High Level and ran up the western side of the Taff valley. It joined the ex-V of N branch at Joint Line Junction about 1 1/4 miles from High Level.

An unidentified 2-8-0T heads a westbound freight out of Quakers Yard High Level towards the 703yd long Quakers Yard tunnel and onwards to Aberdare. On the left hand side of the picture can be seen signals for the TVR's Cardiff-Merthyr line through the Low Level station. The viaduct which can be seen before the entrance to Quakers Yard tunnel and the viaduct on the adjacent Merthyr line at Quakers Yard both suffered from subsidence, and for many years the arches were shored up with heavy timbers, trains on both lines being subject to a 10mph speed restriction.

Left: 0-6-2T No 6605 approaches Mountain Ash from Aberdare with a Neath to Pontypool Road train on 7 July 1962. The buses on the top right hand side of the picture belonged to the Red & White bus company, the leading vehicle being identified as a 1950s Leyland Tiger with a Lydney Coachworks body. On the left side of the picture the winding gear of the NCB's Mountain Ash colliery can be seen.

A characteristic of this route was its switchback gradients and civil engineering features. In the course of its route from Pontypool to Neath it ran along four river valleys, spanned a further four rivers and crossed three water-sheds. Throughout the line steep gradients and massive embankments were the order of the day. To achieve this the line required four tunnels and three viaducts, the latter including those at Hengoed and Crumlin. Whilst the unique viaduct at Crumlin was scheduled for preservation its ageing fabric deteriorated and it had to be dismantled.

Right: Another Neath-Pontypool Road train is featured at Mountain Ash, this time behind 0-6-0PT No 9796 as it leaves the GWR Cardiff Road station on 31 May 1962. On the right is the River Cynon and beyond that the NCB colliery. Where a convenient loop in the River Cynon produced a little extra width, both the Taff Vale and the Great Western built their stations within a few yards of each other on opposite banks of the river. In addition to this, their goods yards were adjacent and at one time a connection linked the stations. The whole railway complex was also sandwiched between Nixon's Navigation and Deep Duffryn collieries which were less than half a mile apart.

Four classes of tank locomotive are featured in this picture taken inside the roundhouse at Aberdare (86J) MPD on 3 August 1959. The shed at Aberdare owed its position at the head of the Cynon valley to its nearness to junctions with the Dare Valley and Merthyr branches, as well as being located at the largest town between Pontypool and Neath. Whilst one's perception of the railways of South Wales is entirely one of industrial lines serving mines and steelworks, it does obscure the fact that some railways took on a more rural aspect. Much of the land in the Cynon Valley could no longer produce hay, so this had to be imported from places like Cowbridge to satisfy the needs of pit ponies and delivery horses.

Of the countless thousands of coal trains to leave Aberdare, one in particular deserves a mention. It left at 9.50am on 9 January 1886 and its consist was 14 laden coal wagons and two brake vans, its destination Salisbury. Routed over the LNWR branch at Pontllanfraith to avoid the congestion at Pontypool it was in fact the first train to use the Severn Tunnel, essentially being a trial run some nine months before the official opening. The depot at Aberdare closed completely from 1 March 1965. *Trevor B. Owen*

Recently returned from a Heavy Intermediate overhaul at Caerphilly Factory, 0-6-2T No 6622 is seen under the coaler at Aberdare MPD on 14 October 1962. Completed at Swindon Factory in January 1928 at a cost of £3,841, which included £858 for the boiler, it was initially allocated to Cardiff Cathays MPD although one month later was despatched to Barry. A powerful Collett design dating from 1924, it was based on the dimensions of the Rhymney Railway's 'R' Class. At the time of this picture the class was designated 5MT by BR, this loco carrying a plain green livery rather than the official lined black. *W. Potter*

Left: 0-6-0PT No 6416 has arrived at Abernant with a Merthyr-Hirwaun auto working on 31 May 1962. The line's major engineering feat was the construction of the Merthyr Tunnel. Together with heavy earthworks in the Taff Valley, the line took six years to build and bankrupted two contractors, the opening being delayed until 2 November 1853. Despite its lowly status Brunel contrived to stamp his personality on the line, the station at Abernant originally having tall chimneys decorated in the Italian style, complete with campaniles, very similar to those at Chippenham when originally built.

Above: The second railway to enter the Afan valley was the GWR. Its extension to the Llynfi & Ogmore Railway from Nantyffyllon to Cymmer opening in 1878 together with mineral extensions to Abergwynfi. Here, 0-6-0PT No 8721 arrives at Abergwynfi with a train from Bridgend on 3 August 1959. The passenger service was withdrawn from 13 June 1960, although the line behind the platform to Avon Colliery remained in use for another nine years. *Trevor B. Owen*

0-6-0PT No 4669 arrives at Tondu with an Abergwynfi -Bridgend train on 2 June 1962, the station having two platforms on the Porthcawl and Bridgend lines. The line to the left behind Tondu Middle signalbox leads to the Llynfi valley and that to the right to the Ogmore and Garw valleys. Behind the locomotive depot another line linked these two forming a triangle.

The branch to Porthcawl started at Tondu and although easily graded south of the GWR main line at Pyle it was extremely tortuous. Such were the gradients the Great Western and later BR (up to 1952) kept one or two of the small '44XX' Class at Tondu to work the line. Another peculiar practice adopted by the shed staff at Tondu from about 1925 was to send out the

regular two '44XX' tanks bunker to bunker and on their return to Tondu each would be reversed. This odd practice was implemented to even out flange wear even on these small locomotives. Today the loco shed has been demolished, the sidings are lifted and only the running lines remain.
John Wiltshire

Hudswell Clarke 0-6-0ST No 618 *Antonia* of 1902 pauses between shunting operations at the NCB drift mine at Penllwyngwent, two-thirds of the way up the Ogmore Valley. The line passing Penllwyngwent was the GWR line from Tondu to Ogmore Vale and Nantymoel. In addition to the usual pannier tanks, the line was also worked by auto-fitted 2-6-2Ts and remained open to passenger traffic until 5 May 1958.

Left: The crew of 0-6-0PT No 9796 prepare to depart from Neath (Riverside) with the 11.25am(SO) to Brecon on 6 October 1962. The overbridge carries the South Wales main line. The Neath & Brecon Railway was incorporated as the Dulais Valley Railway by an Act of Parliament dated 29 July 1862. By 13 July 1863 the railway had expanded and an additional act changed its title to the Neath & Brecon Railway. This latter act gave the railway powers to extend northwards over the mountains to Devynock and through the Vale of Usk to Brecon. In May 1885 the N&B was honoured with the patronage of the world-famous opera singer Adelina Patti who had purchased the castle at Craig-y-Nos and had converted it for her home. For her eminent guests a special waiting room was built on what had been the bare down platform . *John Wiltshire*

Above: Nearing the end of its operational life, the corrugated four-track straight shed at Pantyffynon is depicted on 31 May 1963. Pantyffynon was the junction for the Brynamman branch, and was served by trains from Swansea, Llanelly and Shrewsbury. In addition to local goods a considerable tonnage of coal traffic was raised from several pits in the area, all providing work for the depot. *John Wiltshire*

BR Standard Class 4 2-6-4T No 80097 departs from Pontardulais Junction with 10.55am train to Swansea (Victoria) on 31 May 1963, the level crossing in the foreground restraining road traffic over the A48 main road to West Wales. The railway from Swansea to Pontardulais and the single line branch to Llanmorlais formed the southern section of what became the well-known Central Wales line of the LNWR. The most distinctive feature at Pontardulais was its footbridge which spanned all four platforms, two of these serving the line to Llanelly and the other two, the line to Swansea. Diverging at Pontardulais, the Swansea section was 12¹/₂ miles long and initially ran through an industrial landscape of steelworks and pit workings. However, beyond Dunvant the scenery changed dramatically as the line dropped through the attractive Clyne Woods before it encountered the sea shore beyond Mumbles Road station. Today the line from Pontardulais to Swansea is the only section of the Central Wales route to have been closed, Swansea traffic now working via Llanelli. *John Wiltshire*

Also on 31 May 1963 at Pontardulais Junction, 0-6-0PT No 4676 is being prepared to depart with the 11.5am service to Llanelly. In its formative years the line to Llanelly belonged to the Llanelly Railway & Dock Co, which over a number of years flirted with both the GWR and the LNWR. However, the company found itself divided between the two, the end result being that the LNWR took the Pontardulais-Swansea section, the GWR taking the rest. This resulted in LNWR trains having to pass over GWR metals between Llandilo and Pontardulais in order to reach Swansea (Victoria). *John Wiltshire*

PONTARDULAIS JUNCTION
CHANGE FOR
LLANELLY

Left: A delightful picture of former P. & M. Peckett 0-4-0ST No 1152 as it traverses the connecting line from the former Midland line to the Swansea dock complex on 10 September 1959. On the top right hand side of the picture can be seen the site of Swansea St Thomas and on the left is the River Tawe.
John Wiltshire

Above: Taken on the same day as the previous picture, sister 0-4-0ST No 1151 threads the Swansea South Dock complex near Weavers Mill with its one wagon load, progress being supervised by a pilotman and its cab bell ringing to warn traffic of its approach. On withdrawal of Nos 1151 and 1152, former GWR No 1338 was allocated to East Dock shed in 1960 to continue duties there. This reallocation was necessary because of the requirement for a short wheel-base loco to shunt certain low-level lines around the South Dock. No 1338 continued these duties until it was withdrawn in September 1963 when it was the last survivor of the GWR standard gauge constituent engines.
John Wiltshire

Following the departure of GWR No 1338 into preservation at the Bleadon Railway Museum, the next loco to be imported to work the lines into Swansea South Dock was former LMS 0-4-0ST No 47003 which is seen here crossing the swingbridge from Swansea East Dock on 9 September 1963. Other non-GWR types which later arrived to cover these duties included former Midland Railway 0-4-0ST No 41535 and former L&Y 0-4-0ST No 51218. Today the landward half of the swingbridge still remains as does the grey building in the left background. The red building on the right was a hydraulic pump house and has now been converted into a 'Beefeater' steakhouse, appropriately named the 'Pump House' restaurant. These modernisations are all part of the intensively developed Marina & Holiday complex which occupies the former South Docks area. The site to the left of the picture today is the Swansea Industrial Museum. *John Wiltshire*

BR Standard Class '4' 2-6-4T No 80099 leaves Swansea Bay with the 9.45am Swansea (Victoria)-Shrewsbury on 25 May 1963. The stretch of line from Mumbles Road station to Swansea Bay provided the operating department with one of their most unusual problems — that of keeping the sand off the tracks. One thing that could be guaranteed from the exposed wooden structure at Swansea Bay was a surefooted start. Just before the line entered Swansea (Victoria) it swung inland with connections to the high-level lines, South Dock and Paxton Street shed.
John Wiltshire

Left: An unidentified BR Standard Class '4' 2-6-4T prepares for departure from Gowerton (South) with an evening train for Swansea on 31 May 1963. From Gowerton South branched the lonely line to Llanmorlais on the north Gower coast. Some 4¾ miles in length, this branch was partly constructed over the abandoned Penclawdd Canal which had closed in 1814. Opening for passengers and freight in January 1868 the line was acquired by the LNWR in September 1873 and was extended to Llanmorlais, a distance of two miles on 1 March 1884. The pre-Grouping train service consisted of six trains per day with an extra on Saturdays, but fell victim to competing bus services and was closed by the LMS on 5 January 1931. Originally opened to serve mineral interests in the area, freight traffic continued under BR until 2 September 1957. Today part of the line from Llanmorlais to Crofty is an informal footpath, the station house at Llanmorlais is still in existence while that at Penclawdd has been restored as a house. *John Wiltshire*

Above: Andrew Barclay 0-4-0ST No 1276/12 *Nora* is seen at work inside the melting shop at Llanelly Steel Works on 10 June 1967. Because of the limited clearances inside the works and this locomotive spending much of its operational life under cover, it was not necessary to fit it with a cab.

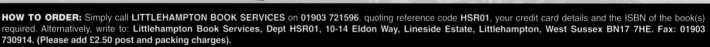